WHO LIVES ON THE MOON (MOON FACTS): SECOND GRADE GEOGRAPHY SERIES

Speedy Publishing LLC
40 E. Main St. #1156
Newark, DE 19711
www.speedypublishing.com

**The Moon is Earth's
only natural satellite.**

The Moon
is about 4.5
billion years
old. The
surface is
covered in
craters, pits
and scars.

The first
spacecraft
to reach the
moon was
"Luna I"
in 1959
which was a
soviet craft
launched by
the USSR.

Neil Armstrong was the very first person, to put his footsteps onto the lunar surface. He stepped out of his spacecraft, the Eagle, on 21 July 1969.

The moon
orbits the
Earth, it is also
spinning at
the same time.
The moon
takes about 29
days to orbit
the Earth.

The moon has no atmosphere. Temperatures on the moons surface can range from a freezing -123°C to a boiling 123°C.

The moon has a mountainous landscape. The tallest range is called the Montes Apenninus.

There is an American flag on the moon. Neil Armstrong planted it there during the first moon landing.

www.ingramcontent.com/pod-product-compliance
Lightning Source LLC
Chambersburg PA
CBHW080947130726
48003CB00010BA/3128